Let's Talk Podcasting
for kids

AMANDA CUPIDO

Let's Talk Podcasting for Kids
Published and owned by: Let's Talk Podcasting Inc.
Copyright © 2025 by Amanda Cupido
All rights reserved
Printed in Canada

No part of this book may be used or reproduced in any manner whatsoever without written permission except in the case of brief quotations embodied in critical articles and reviews. For more information or to write to the publisher, please email info@letstalkpodcasting.com.

ISBN is 978-1-0690898-3-0

Illustrated and designed by Ladan Lajevardi
Publishing support by Ishitaa Chopra

For Clementine, Rafael and Eliana—may you grow up to love podcasting as much as I do.

And for Brooks—this book's first fan.

I have made more than 50 different shows! Not all of them were for me. Most of them were for other people.

I like helping people make podcasts. I also like helping people learn about podcasts.

Happy Birthday Podcast

Did you know podcasts were invented in 2004? That means they are much older than you!

In the beginning, podcasts were audio recordings of people talking, with no pictures. You could listen to them by streaming and downloading podcasts from the internet.

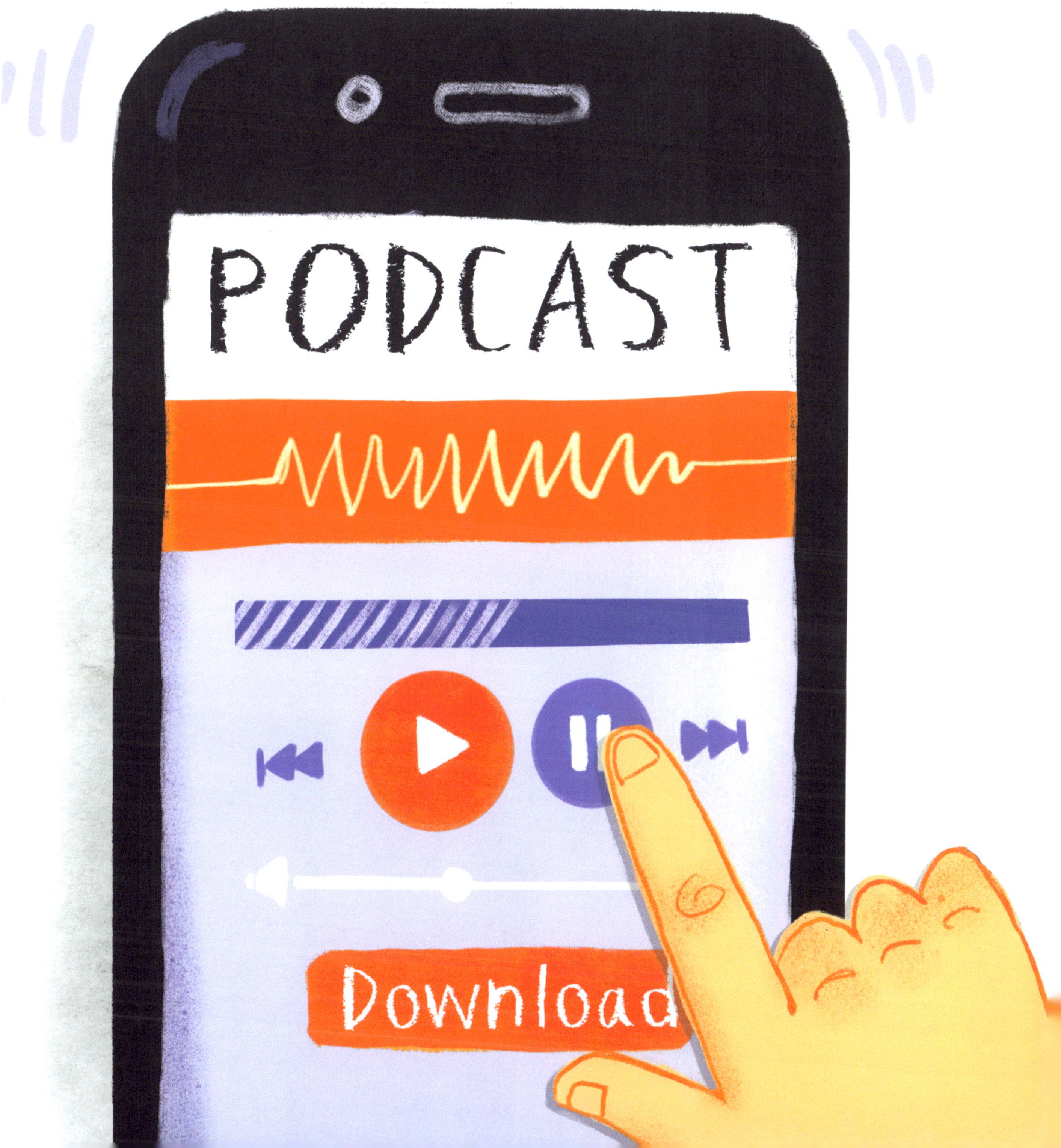
PODCAST
Download

The word podcast is a combination of the words iPod and broadcast. iPods were devices to play music and audio. Broadcast refers to sharing stories on the radio or television.

The definition of podcast keeps changing. Now there are also video podcasts on the internet.

If you want to make a podcast, first you need to come up with a theme for your show.

What do you want it to be about?

Nature?
Food?
Your family?

Next you need to decide who will be speaking on the podcast.

Is it just you?
Will you have a co-host?
Will there be guests?

17

Then you need to choose how many episodes you will make.

Will it be 1 episode? 5 episodes? 10 episodes?

After that, you have to plan what you will talk about. Pick a topic for each episode. For example, if your show is about your family, you might have one episode about each member of your family.

Now it's time to record! You can use a tablet, computer or even a phone to capture the story. Sometimes people even perform podcasts on a stage in front of an audience.

You can ask questions like:

Why is family important?

How do you show you care?

What is your favourite thing to do together?

Then, you can share your podcast or just keep it for yourself.

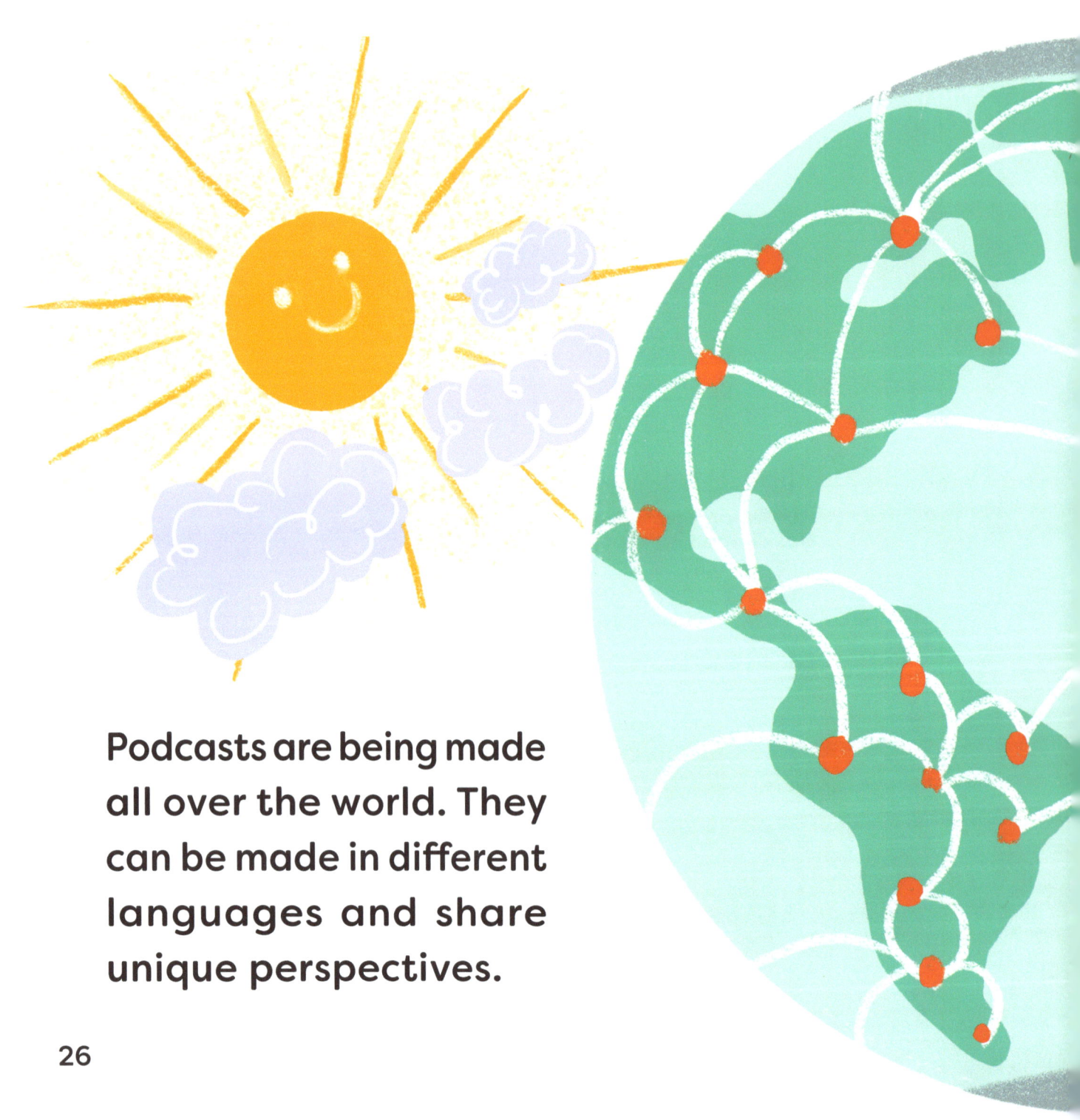

Podcasts are being made all over the world. They can be made in different languages and share unique perspectives.

Podcasts allow people to share their stories. I believe everyone has a story that's worth telling.

So what story are you going to tell?

THE END

What is the name of your podcast?

Who will be your guests?

What questions you will ask?

www.ingramcontent.com/pod-product-compliance
Lightning Source LLC
LaVergne TN
LVHW071652060526
838200LV00029B/436